Streets of Trees

Streets of Trees

of

Trees

A COLLECTION OF POEMS FROM THE
HOLDERNESS VERSE MAKER

The Holderness
Verse Maker

Dedication

I would like to dedicate this book to you,

a person who has given it your precious time,

Also to my mother and father for without

them these words would not be.

Table of Contents

Why This Dejection?

There's pain in my heart and strife in my head,
When I start the day and when I go to bed,
What do I do and where do I go?
Who should I be and what should I know?

Can I tell all my friends? Will they understand?
Am I truly alone? Is that what he planned?
If I knock on the door,
And stand patient in awe,
Will he welcome me in and tell what it's all for?

Pain in my heart, will you please turn to peace?
When I look through the window, then maybe I'll see,
Others who walk in a chaos of life,
Others who know of the anguish of strife.

Pain in our hearts and these thoughts in our head,
Many do have them and take them to bed,
We have no one to tell, but everyone knows,
That, I'm afraid, is just how it goes.

Economy of Life

Do we all really know what we all really need?
If we all need a lot, is it merely our greed?
Is it better for us, the devil we know?
And we merely accept, and go with the flow?

From all of these questions that we always ask,
We should know that contentment should be our main task,
For all of us life is all that we have,
That is the concept which we all must now grasp.

All of us, different, that's what we're taught,
And we're told that contentment can sometimes be bought,
But as we are still all gaining more,
We are all as lost as we were before.

Life is all we have, it's true,
In the end, there is just you.
If we make it, if we fail,
We have life, that fact prevails.

Live like this or live like that,
That's what they've said throughout the past,
You need these or you need those,
Buy these books or wear these clothes,
Your life is yours and yours alone,
Yours to cherish, yours to grow,
Bear in mind, same goes for all,
Live your life until you fall.

Night of the Epiphany

Sounds in the distance, the ringing of bells,
Maybe from heaven, maybe from hell,
Embracing the rhythm, embracing the sound,
As I get closer and get lost in the crowd,
My heart starts to pound and my thoughts start to race,
Trembling treble and thundering bass,
People surround me, feral and raw,
Why did they not talk about this before?

Arms and heads racing and thrashing around,
Possessed by the animal trapped in the sound,
The drums pull my strings, like a puppet I move,
To an insane, magnificent, apocalypse groove.
The army of crazies are out in full swing,
And louder and louder the bells start to ring.

I close my eyes as I relish the bliss,
The energy fills me as I clench my fists,
Against the air I bang my head,
I march unperturbed in the army of death,
Tonight I awaken, tonight I'm alive,
The morning to steal it when it soon arrives,
But times like this you don't forget,
And these are things I won't regret.

Look at my eyes, look at my face,
Tomorrow I will be leaving this place,
I'll remember the kindred, the army at night,
Soldiering through till we met with the light,
We'll always remember the night that is gone,
Wishing for one more before life is done.

The Guide

Listen to the angel in your life,
It is the one who's always been,
Through your anger, pain and strife,
Always there but never seen,
If it's war or if it's peace,
Old nightmares or new childhood dreams,
Listen to the voice inside,
Always whispers, never screams.

Angel's there to let you know,
To always prosper, always grow,
To cast your sight upon the things,
Which are good and that will bring,
Brand new hope to realise,
When looking through the angel's eyes,
That you mattered from the start,
Hear angels say it to the heart.

Wherever you are, and this means you,
Listen to me, sail on through,
Spread your wings and welcome peace,
Cast your devil to the sea.

The Acolytes

Strange to me and for a few,

How our lives began with you,

How your music made us grow,

Into the people you now know.

Your rhythmic waves, upon our sea,

Carried us to where we're free.

In a cafe, in the park,

You carry up our lonely hearts.

We see each other now and then,

One with guitar, one with pen,

Trying to reply to you,

But it's always been us few.

I see you peering out at us,

From the window of a bus.

Knowing that we'll never start,

Or end to know a breaking heart.

Live in the Dream

Now that I return from work,
Music spirals round,
Now it's time to scribe the beats,
Capturing the sound.
In this room, a rhythm rolls,
Filling heart and head,
Now I write this thought for you,
Dreaming from my bed.

Can I take you on a ride?
If I can, then read,
Through my day and through the night,
Through my head of dreams,
Dreams, evoked,

I hope, in you,
Be they big or small,
Tune in, read my thoughts and prayers,
My dusk until my dawn.

Music guides my mind and soul,
As you have grown to know,
Step into a distant land,
Together let us grow.
Together we will know the beat,
Of dreams that are played there,
Together in our distant land,
That is our place of prayer.
Pray for things that are to come,
The things that we forgot,
Things that bring us closer,
And, let us lose them not.

A Journey of Solitude

Hi, how are you today
On my river roll.
Nice to meet you finally,
You're back in control.
Upstream are some people waiting,
People from your dream,
And there are some old friends around,
When you ride downstream.

There you are again, let go,
Please don't be confused,
The boat can't sink or be capsized,
It only carries you.

If you must get back to shore,
This you cannot do,
Not until the river ends,
And there you find the truth.

To You, My Friend

Are you available? It's only me,

Can we talk about you? Or maybe, we?

Are you available in your day,

Upon this planet where we must stay?

Are you happy to take time out

Of a schedule you can do without?

Of another mundane boring task?

If not, fine, I thought I'd ask,

Do you like music, or the beach?

Or the forest, and the trees?

Where do you go when you want to dream?

What makes you laugh? When do you scream?

Just thought I'd ask, just so I know,

The one who I want to now see grow,

And while you grow, to cherish life,
Single, husband, or a wife,
Son or daughter, there you are,
Wishing on our shining star,
Sharing time just me and you,
We learnt to get each other through,
So when you're sick, or tired or poor,
I stand with you throughout it all.

The Uphill Posse

Crazy army, keep on marching,
March on up towards the drum,
We are all barmy and just starting,
Moving to our kingdom come.

Every day we are all losing minds,
But gain a little soul,
Crazy people, barmy kin,
March on as we lose control.

Sound the trumpet and the bells,
Come, my army, march,
The darkness we have overcome,
And awe rests in our hearts.

Shout and sing and dance along
Up and up we go,
Let's go to where we all belong,
Where is it? Well, who knows?

March in darkness, march in light,
We must be insane.
Even in the surly night,
The crazy army reign.

An Ocean of Euphoria

"Wake up, wake up," she said to me,
Whilst my mind was sailing 'cross the sea,
"Do you want to die like this?
Go whilst living mortal bliss?"

"Wake up now, you're late for school.
Do you really want to be a fool?
Wake up now, it's time for work.
Get your head on, be alert."

If I'm lazy, I don't care,
It doesn't matter, the clothes I wear,
The place I live, the car I drive,
When I relax I feel alive,

When I'm alive, I don't need
To work and work until I bleed,
I'm content to be just me,
Sailing through upon the sea.

Please don't take me from my dream,
Please be nice and leave me be,
My euphoric mystery,
Where I'm carried to be free.

A Thought of Generosity

I think about it all the time,
What's the answer to this life?
When people really never care,
We must be good but nothing's there,
We must be helpful to our kin,
We must be kind and then we'll win,
But when we're kind, they only take,
And then we feel it's a mistake.

Whatever you think, I think too,
So you are me and I am you,
"What's the answer?" we both ask,
But neither know; it comes to pass.

When we forget to think and see,
That I am you and you are me,
And all we both can do is take,
It's who we are, make no mistake.

How's Things, My Friend?

Thanks for coming, now you're here,

Get some food and grab a beer,

Talk about what's going to come,

Where we've been and what we've done,

We've been together for a long time,

Done things that should be called crime,

Laughed and cried along the way,

But friends we both will always stay,

We know each other oh so well,

Enough to give the other hell,

Without you, I'd be alone,

Without you, life would not be home.

Thanks for your ear and for your time,

It's good to hear you're doing fine.

Do Not Disturb

Telephone noise desists my peace,

The surly sound makes me uneased.

Who is it, not the police?

Someone to tell me I'm diseased?

Is it my boss and I've got to work,

Or someone who wants to shout and curse?

Or is it someone who wants my cash,

Or my time or my soul or to dwell on my past?

There it is, now on vibrate.

On the other end, I'll meet my fate.

Is it a hoax? Is it a prank?

An annoying person from the bank?

Whoever it is, please let them know,

Just fuck off, leave me alone.

Live It Up

Live today, die tomorrow,
Love your brilliant life.
Live for what you love to do,
And never live for strife.
Live for autumn, summer, spring,
Live for winter too.
Live for all the songs you sing,
And beauty that you view.

Live today for all you love,
Make your kindred proud.
Live for cosy Sunday mornings,
Live for parties loud.
Live for all your favourite memories,
Live them out again,
Love and live until you're gone,
Till heavens you are sent.

The State of Trepidation

It will happen, that's for sure, whatever it may be,

That is what you say to you and what you say to me.

So I listen, so do you; we lock ourselves away,

It will happen, that's for sure, but maybe not today.

When it happens, oh my lord, the terror and the pain,

Even though I know it didn't happen yesterday.

If you could really tell the future, then, so for sure can I,

And if it hasn't happened yet, then it may be a lie.

Which Way Next?

Pain is gone,

A saxophone plays,

The sax, then piano,

As daylight fades,

Where do I go?

Rhythm guides,

Through the days,

And through the nights.

Let's Write a Story

What are you doing?

What did you do?

We are here and you are too,

Bound together in the world,

Fish within a pool,

Sometimes talk about the weather,

Or maybe start a duel,

Sometimes humans, maybe monkeys,

Maybe lions, sometimes sharks,

But what we're in, we're in together,

Tall, short, light or dark.

We together have a story,

Letters in a book,

Once you gave me something nice,

Then you gave a funny look.

Once I tripped you up and smiled,
Once you tripped me too,
That story's written, the next is not,
Where did you go? What did you do?

The Sombre Angel

She believed that she could fly,
She told me many years ago,
Stupid, yes, you can't deny,
I was about to say goodbye and go.
She had a pair of angel's wings,
Tattooed on her back,
I stayed to laugh at stupid things,
But I gave a little slack.
"So you can fly with those?" I asked,
"Those little tattooed wings?
And where do you suppose you'll go?
Have you thought about these things?"

"Well," she said, "When I take off
And I fly up high,
I'll see there's nothing in this world
So, I'll just crash and die."

That's Life

Gotta get up,
Sleep in my eyes.
Where was I last night?
I was out with the guys.
I remember the beers,
And remember the shots,
And then what happened?
Shit, I drank lots.
And where did we go
After the pub?
My head is killing.
Did we go to a club?

Now I sit up in bed,
And I look around.
There is only me,
And an annoying sound.

A clock shows half three,
And I'm all alone,
Tell me someone, tell me now,
Please, how do I get home?

Look out the window,
Look at the cars,
I should be at work,
But my head is on Mars.
What should I do?
I just don't know,
The boss will go crazy,
I should quickly go.

A knock on the door,
A yell: "Are you there?"
I shout out, "Yes, I'm here
Still in underwear."
The voice shouts, "Get dressed now, dear,
For no man do they wait
The end of life has now transpired,
So come now, meet your fate."

Back on My Own

Goodbye, old friends, I never said,
But where have you all gone?
So many of you yesterday,
But one day there'll be none.

Good friends, I call, where are you now?
You are still in my heart,
But no more do I see you all,
Oh, why did you depart?

When I'm older, I pray to you,
That I do not forget,
The smiles upon your faces and
The times when we first met.

If I listen hard enough,
I hear your voices sing,
And in those times, I will remember,
Together we have been.

What Was Your Crime?

Listen, prisoner of the mind,

I wish that they could see,

When they said malicious words to you,

They stopped you being free.

Why is it that they could not see

The prison they created?

And left you in there, all alone,

Why was it you they hated?

Hated you for love of peace,

Prisoner of the mind,

And then they took it out on you,

When theirs they could not find.

Please don't learn to hate them now,
As you live there all alone,
Find your love and peace again,
Make your cell your home.

We can all be free again,
Prisoner of the mind,
Learn to live for you again,
Life is there for you to find.

Crossing Paths

Wave hello, say goodbye,
There's a sparkle in your eye.
First look east, then north, south, west,
But here with you is always best.

Hello, we say and then embrace,
Then we shake hands, then on our way.
Whether it's east, west, south or north,
Time together took its course.

When we meet up once again,
Doing shopping, on the plane,
We realise another time,
Forever won't be yours and mine.

We say hello but why? I ask,
Goodbye is not our final task,
Just a temporary change of scene,
To reminisce on time that's been.

Never To Be Known

Words, yes words, too hard to say,
Before I say them, you're away,
Away with words, words of your own,
Forever, words to me, unknown.

Secrets sometimes should be kept,
When they were shared, then tears were wept,
Words, just words, too hard to say,
Secrets keep, with us they stay.

Will I see the things you do?
Will we ever know the truth?
Some reality we miss,
Because some words won't leave our lips.

A False Sense of Belonging

"One coffee please." Only one.
That is where it all began,
Just me, myself, I and my drink,
I took some time and had a think.

I looked round at the lonely view,
What do people in here do?
On their laptops or on the phone,
But every one of them, alone,
All alone and just like me,
Is this how I'm supposed to be?

"No way," I told myself that day,
"I can't ever be this way."
I left my coffee and walked out,
I didn't have a slight of doubt,
I wandered and went for a beer,
Outside the pub I heard a cheer.

I went inside and laughter rang,
Throughout the air the jukebox sang,
"Is this where I'm supposed to be?"
I ask myself, "Now is this me?"
I had a beer and then one more,
Another few, then hit the floor.
Landlord said I have to leave,
So nothing more had been achieved.

Lonely still, next day I thought,
Of all the coffee and beer I'd bought,
Just to pass the time away,
Just another lonely day.

All Alone... Don't Care

Where, I pray, did love go?
What, I ask, went wrong?
Can I see it through the window?
Don't miss it though, it's gone.

I'm told that love is everything,
It inspires to write and sing,
But I'm just fine the way I am,
I'm good with not being a sham.

She loves me, she loves me not,
Is really all that some have got,
I can't say that it makes me sick,
But it doesn't bother me one bit.

I can't fathom, those who love,
And think it's sent from God above,
And worry 'bout their lonely heart,
That just as easily could consume art,
Music, writing and solitude.
I really don't mean to be rude.
I just can't think of life that way,
Hurting for nothing every day.

Love is something I don't seek,
But I'd never say it's weak,
I'm never lonely when I sleep,
You very rarely see me weep.

Have a Safe Flight

Clear the runway, time to fly.

Take off and cruise until I die,

1, 2, 3, 4, here I go,

Persist through rain, sleet, hail and snow.

Thrust into life as we now know.

And where we're going, none do know,

The runway cleared by ones we love,

Path is set by God above.

When to take off is our right,

To choose by day or maybe night.

We must now go and keep our path,
Don't deviate, avoid the wrath,
Listen to your favourite tune,
And fly your plane beneath the moon.

Clear the runway, here we go,
Our aircraft carrying our souls,
Cruising through the sky so fast,
And hope, for a while, our rides will last.

One Night in June

I saw her get her car and go.

Where she was going I did not know.

I met her first, you know, in June

When we danced beneath the moon.

It's August now and I'm alone,

My solitude has grown and grown.

As I watched her drive away,

I knew that in my mind she'd stay.

Her smile, I know, I can't forget.

The thing I saw when we first met,

The smile that shone like gold in June,

The smile that danced beneath the moon.

Tears filled my eyes, now she was gone,
And from my sky I'd lost the sun
I sang away a lonely tune,
A song I heard one night in June.

The Place Where You Come From

Origins of life and thought,
We were created, love we sought,
Origins of thought and life,
Are they in her lover? In his wife?
We seek our parents' DNA,
Our family trees, the god we pray,
We seek the history of the earth,
We seek divine and noble birth,
To origins we may feel blind,
Just feeling we've been left behind.

The origin of life is love,
Feeling that we're from above,
Origins of thought is life,
To be living is to strive,
To strive is to do with care,
Care for those, who're always there.
Are there now, were there before,
Before they strived with us in store.
With us in store, their love and strife,
Were origins of thought and life.

Don't Get the Fever

Fever growing all around,

Still no bodies hit the ground,

Will an antidote appear

And the air again be clear?

Fever taking all control,

First the mind and the soul,

Affecting those who can't be told,

Kills the young and saves the old.

Raise a glass and make a toast,

To the king we love the most,

Crush the fever in his land

Then our souls will not be damned.

Fever knocking on the door,
Don't come here now anymore,
We've cast our differences aside
So fever won't eat us alive.

Fever, we will see you die,
When we finally say goodbye,
Then our world again we own,
Fever won't again be known,
Children once again will sing,
Church bells once again will ring,
Then the past will be the past
Please don't let the fever last.

Better believe it, don't get the fever.

A Point of Animosity

When we meet for the first time,

It may be the last,

It depends how I feel,

And soon may come to pass.

My friends can be enemies,

And enemies, friends,

So don't be offended,

I don't like to pretend.

When we met up,

What did we say?

We wasted some time,

And then went away,

To our goals and our lives,
Our nightmares and dreams,
Then we met for a while,
So pointless, it seems.

When I can only
Trust in myself,
What good are you,
But to squander my wealth.
It's just how I feel,
So don't get me wrong,
It's part of my soul,
My life's bitter song.

Looking for what?
Someone to hate?
Don't like the fact?
Well, you've heard it's too late.

In Search of a Career

Train at this, train at that,
It's the rules and that's a fact.
Be a cleaner, be a cook,
They'll never give a second look.
Do it now until you die
If you're lucky you'll get by.
What you must be in this life
Is a husband or a wife.
Trained at this or trained at that,
On the back you'll get a pat.

Your boss will never let you go,
At least that's what they tell you so.
You started out as the trainee,
And that's all you'll ever be.

If you're lucky you'll escape,
But we are not taught to be brave.
Keep your head down, toe the line,
Shut your mouth and you'll be fine.
Know to never answer back
And always train at this and that.

One day you can maybe see,
They only want to crush your dreams,
With the pointless this and pointless that,
Stupid pats upon the back.
This world was not meant to be,
We don't belong here, you and me.
We dream of a place somewhere else,
We make a toast to our good health.
Time's been wasted, what to do?
Let's just get each other through.
We're here together in the end,
So let's remember that we're friends.

Want What You Can Have

Change in my life,

I need to embrace.

Things I can't have,

I don't need to chase.

If I want what I can't have,

I can't have what I want,

If I want what I can,

I will have what I sought.

Living in flux,

Things lost and gained.

I can't control changes,

But I'll not be ashamed.

Change can't be fought,
What's done is done,
Some lessons are taught,
When fights can't be won.

Uncertainty is law
I'm afraid that's your lot,
Don't like where you are?
You've got what you've got.
Chaos returns,
That's always the truth,
But, one thing is constant,
You'll always be you.

By being yourself,
What more could you be?
Change your perspective,
Then you can be free.
So want what you can,
And have what you want.
That is the lesson,
That all should be taught.

What To Do Today

Is it fine to find free time?

Time to love or lose?

And, is it fine to drink some wine,

Or should we quit the booze?

Is the day beginning well,

Or is the rhythm lost?

At the end of the day, will I drink again?

And if so, what's the cost?

Someone, somewhere thinks like me,

They are lonely too,

They laugh and cry into a glass,

Can we get each other through?

Ease my burden, o' sweet time,
Help me through again,
Maybe I won't drink tonight,
Or maybe if and when.

Help me, someone, rise above.
I think of wine, you think of love,
Who is right, who is wrong?
Is drunkenness where I belong?
Is it fine to find free time?
Time to live and love?
Or is it fine just finding time,
To be another drunk?

Back to the Routine

Eat, sleep, work, repeat,

There's always more than that.

Do you seek money, peace or what?

Yes? What to be exact?

Cycling, endless cycling,

Peddling the machine,

And maybe find a little time

To get your washing clean.

Cling to this and cling to that,

Throw this and that away,

But peace and love should be with us,

Throughout the night and day.

Close your eyes and think of those,

Who've blessed you all your life,

When you peddle the machine,
When you hit the strife,
Focus on the things you love,
Not the bits you hate.
Focus on the things you have,
And find a better place.

Posterity of Light

Easy does it, relax your eyes,
Forget the voices that speak lies,
Forget people who drag you down,
Forget the lunacy of town.
Someone wants to know you better,
That is why they wrote this letter,
Someone with a sense of pride,
And admiration for your life.
Someone out there thinks of you,
Watches over all you do,
Do it all again for them,
Then maybe it won't be the same.

It could be me, it could be you,

Either way, you will get through.

Just want to say, just as before,

One day you'll shine forever more.

Look in the mirror, then you'll see,

A person who will be set free,

A person who rejects all lies,

So stand with love beneath our skies.

A Life of Hope

Morning hits me once again,

Hits me with my day,

I hope that this one blesses me,

And that it goes my way.

Please don't let light be malign,

Oh bright sun, through, get me,

Through until the darkness comes,

And in my sleep I'm free.

And in my sleep I dream of light,

Fantasise of day, at night,

But when the morning comes again,

I'm only mocked with threats of pain.

So in the day I dream of night,

And in the night, of day,

Something to look forward to,

Dreams get me through, I pray.

You Are the Melody

Be imbued with music,
The sound that made your soul,
The tunes that shaped your life,
And tones that wrought your mould.
Dance away in presence,
The life that music gave,
The notes that fashioned you,
And led you on your way,
Dulcet songs that fill your life,
That formed your every day,
With our sounds of freedom,
Let's return and always stay.

Traverse the Wild

In this jungle of my mind, what will transpire today?
What will come out from the trees and in this passage stay?
I often see you through the bushes, playing in the rain.
Did you know you live inside this jungle of a brain?

In the jungle you must know that I am never king.
I wander through the plants and vines, and listen to birds sing.
And when they sing those songs, I write down what I hear
for you.
The jungle of a thousand voices, that is the world I view.

Jungle, you are strong and mighty and unpredictable.
Jungle, fill my head and heart till to the brim they're full.
Jungle, guide my hand and soul, what scribe shall be today?
May I, jungle, remain in you, each and every day.

The Mundane Spiral

Going round in circles,
Going round the bend,
The circles never stop, you know,
I don't like it, my friend.
Walking on the treadmill,
Doing it again,
Will it ever end, my lord?
For always it's the same.

Do I settle for these circles?
For when I stop to think,
My mind, it slows my circle down,
And then I start to sink.

So maybe my life's made for circles,
Made for the mundane,
I suppose if someone's getting rich,
The circles numb my brain.

Don't go awry, stay on the treadmill,
Make sure you don't fall,
For if you don't keep in the circle,
You'll have nothing at all.
Outside the circle are the damned,
Inside we're told we're blessed,
So walk in circles constantly,
And hope we pass the test.

Routine, routine, the banter goes,
That's how we all survive,
Pray that the circle doesn't stop,
Or you may lose your life.
And when we're older will the circle,
Still with us, all stay?
Will we all move around in circles,
Until life's called a day?

Hello to you from my neat circle,
Hello to me from yours,
We see each other every day,
Through our circles of chores.
Although we can't get out of them,
We're in our comfort zone,
And if it's circles that you need,
Then you are not alone.

Jazz Up My Day

Put some smooth jazz music on,

Cushion my naked brain,

Put some peace into my heart,

Sunshine through the rain.

Like the rolling of the waves,

It carries me away,

Through the sea of all her dreams,

I ride her through the day.

She sings to me in many voices,

I write down what she says,

She tells me many different stories,

In a plethora of ways.

As she sings to me so sweetly,

Her noise, it fills my sail,

Normally she's gentle,
But sometimes blows a gale,
Play my day away, sweet music,
While I'm here alone,
Make your way inside my head,
And make my heart your home.
Guide my soul throughout the day,
Wherever it may be,
Forever sing your melodies,
Bless me to be free.

Mission Accomplished

Alone in this country,
My head in the clouds,
My spirit is free,
Away from the crowds.
My dawn has now come,
And awoken me,
Under curses of miscreants,
I never shall be.

Alone in the quiet,
Peace has conveyed,
In the moment for which,
I've hoped and I've prayed.

Conduits of bliss
Fill up my soul,
Lighten my load,
And are in control.

Secluded in here,
In the peace of my mind,
Life's pleasures transpire,
And now that I find,
That my life was always,
Looking for me,
To convey to this place,
Where I'll always be free.

Now my eyes, I can close,
And I know I am safe,
I do not need to worry,
Or fear to be brave.
My problems are gone,
At tranquillity's gate,
Enemies are forgotten,
And my mind casts no hate.

I hope and I pray,
I can stay in this place,
To live out my days,
To forfeit the race.
And that here we will be,
All of us one,
To cast out our fears,
While we bask in our sun.

Welcome to the Free World

Iniquity to make them leave
Their homes, their lives and their beliefs,
To westernise forgotten tribes,
To iterate etiquette and lies,
The children were the last to know,
Traditions passed from long ago
Then they were taken from their land
Though all too young to understand.
Wrought in the free world so to speak,
And taught that freedom they shouldn't seek,
And when they spoke their mother tongue,
The teachers beat them one by one.

Iniquity to make them leave,
And teach them western broken dreams,
They were all taught to forget,
The families they'd never met,
And each to live in their new home,
But each of them still on their own,
Thinking of their mother land,
Still too young to understand,
What was the reason they were taken?
The white man surely was mistaken.
I know he doesn't sound like me,
But it's he that he wants me to be.

Like our father, they didn't look,
But without haste from him they took,
His children and his way of life,
Unto forced labour, abuse and strife.
We children never realised,
That we were being westernised,
But from the start we could clearly see,
Second-class citizens we'd always be.

Enough To Make You Crazy

Understand your place,
Know what you should do,
Understand the race,
Make sure you get through.
If you don't get through,
Then you may get lost,
And if you lose your way,
Then your life it may cost.
Keep up with the leaders,
Think upon their lines,
Always do your homework,
Avoid hefty fines.

Read and work, learn all you can,

Take lessons that are taught,

Listen to your teachers,

Make yourself well wrought.

Run and run, yes run the race,

Maybe you'll retire,

Until then please now know your place,

To keep out of the fire.

Don't you let the big man down,

Or find yourself run out of town,

There you can't rejoin the masses,

Who just keep running whilst the time passes.

Keep your head, don't do too much,

But do all you can,

Keep on doing the good work,

I hope you understand.

Get a routine, one that works,

Repeat it every day,

Remember take some time to rest,

And also time to play.

Do it your way, do it theirs,
It's enough to drive you mad,
But if you just keep going, then,
With all your toil, be glad.

Finding Purpose

I sometimes wonder why I write,

And why it keeps me up at night,

Is it for me? Or for you?

Is that all that I can do?

Possibly I do because,

If there is no God above,

Then my writing is my prayer,

Still hoping that something is there,

Hoping that someone will read,

And see my life of being me,

Hoping that some of us share,

The hope and dream that just out there

Are others who are like us too,

That all share in all our earthly view,

That while we're trapped here in this place,
We see that we don't need to fight and race,
But take time out to share a thought,
To laugh and cry, as we've been taught.
Thank you for accompanying me,
In our boat upon our sea.

Nature's Rhythm

Listen to the pouring rain,
Falling on your face,
No longer feel regret or pain,
No longer be disgrace.
The clock is ticking, listen now,
The process can't be fought,
Be at one with time itself,
At one be with this thought.

Listen to the falling rain,
Feel it comfort you.
Listen to the sound it makes,
Like colours that you view.

Colours that are in your mind,
Painting every sight,
See your picture, hold it now,
And bless your mind tonight.

There will be thunder, don't shed a care,
Try to set your sight,
On the benign, soft falling rain,
Capturing the light.
Hold on to the memory,
We only have one life,
Grant yourself this moment,
You deserve and have the right.

Cherish the sweet falling rain,
As it falls throughout your days,
Cherish every moment and,
Pray, for a while, it stays.

Us Being Us

I suppose that I'm crazy,
And sometimes a pain,
Overly lazy,
Wear no coat in the rain,
Slurp at my coffee,
Until it sends you mad,
I can't fight myself,
And as me I am glad.

If you have no interest,
No problem, just say,
I don't need your notice,
I'll be swiftly away.
I feel time's not wasted,
But that's only me,
I don't tolerate burdens,
I just like to be free.

Sometimes I get angry,
But it doesn't last,
Don't believe in violence,
Don't dwell on the past.
I don't like the stress,
It just gets in the way,
I'm happy with life,
And I hope that will stay.

My life is right here,
And your life is too,
With our little quirks,
Just me and you.
And *mi fa piacere*,
If we maybe got on,
We don't need to battle,
We've already won.

So if we're all crazy,
And sometimes a pain,
Let's wear it with pride,
For the whole world's insane.

Some Me Time

A fleeting visit somewhere new,
Can I fake being free?
Now I've bought a holiday,
Some time to be me.
But if I'm not me now,
Who am I trying to be?
Someone who lives a fallacy?
For a modest fee?
If I work and work,
To be plastic for one week,
Must I do this all,
Just for me to seek
A place where I won't live,
A life that I won't have,
Although, for a little while,
With things I will be glad.

I suppose that it's not so obscene,
To pretend that I live in a dream.

Manic Depression

Is it destined that I
Now have to stay
In this vibrant and new
Yet lonely a place?
I feel lost and blinded,
By the cruel light,
Have I now fallen from grace?
Subjugated tonight?

The people who're here
Are tenuously good,
But here by myself,
I never could
Be like they are,

Living insane,
So I need to ride
Hard against the grain.
But who's going down?
Why's it only me,
And who then are they
Allowed to be free?

Are they of God?
Or fools in love?
Are they from the gutter?
Or sent from above?
Were they like me?
Or were they born,
Permitted to walk,
Upon the shore?
The shore of their heaven,
The shore of my hell,
The place where I stay,
Alone in my shell.

Manage With Mercy

How do I manage
When the day begins?
Have mercy on me,
If I can't win.
For I don't want
Just to compete,
I want my life,
To be complete.
In the arena,
We're thrown into,
How can I manage
Without you?
Give me mercy,
Please I ask,

Be my rock,
In every task,
See my thoughts,
Let's be one,
Help me manage,
Pain, overcome.

9 781805 416579